FOUR SEASONS OF
BONSAI

FOUR SEASONS OF BONSAI

Kyuzo Murata

Translated by Kate McCandless

KODANSHA INTERNATIONAL
Tokyo • New York • London

Illustration on half-title page: crape myrtle in mid-August.
Illustration on title page: Japanese zelkova in mid-October.

Adapted from *Bonsai no shiki*, originally published in 1984 by Kodansha Ltd.

Distributed in the United States by Kodansha America, Inc., 114 Fifth Avenue, New York, N.Y. 10011, and in the United Kingdom and continental Europe by Kodansha Europe Ltd., 95 Aldwych, London WC2B 4JF. Published by Kodansha International Ltd., 17-14 Otowa 1-chome, Bunkyo-ku, Tokyo 112, and Kodansha America, Inc.

ISBN 4-7700-2120-8
LCC 90-49936

CONTENTS

PREFACE

Every bonsai gardener knows the joys of watching bonsai change through the seasons: a cherry tree in full bloom can be a breathtaking sight, of course, and even evergreens show new growth in spring that matures through summer and fall.

Of the many bonsai books that have appeared in English over the last fifty years, none has really celebrated this integral and rewarding facet of bonsai care. Until now, most books have focused either on teaching the basics of bonsai gardening or on displaying the most famous (and ancient) examples of the art. Of course these endeavors are very important, but I believe it's time to take another step forward and try to create gardens of bonsai that offer more variety and are actually fun to work with throughout the year.

Naturally, many of the bonsai I chose to include in this book are flowering trees, trees that bear fruit, and trees with splendid fall foliage. But this book's seasonal approach has also given me the opportunity to introduce some of the unconventional bonsai that I've been cultivating recently, including grasses, flowers, and other annuals and perennials, which, I've found, are some of the best representatives of seasonal change.

Witness the fern pushing its curled head up through the soil in spring, unfurling its leaves through summer, turning brown in autumn, and dying off in winter, only to send up entirely new shoots in the following spring. What is more dramatic than death and rebirth? And since the literal meaning of "bonsai" is simply "planted in a tray," what is to stop us from applying the principles of tree bonsai to all kinds of plants and flowers as well? Pot a fern in a mound of soil with some moss and you have a miniature forest scene; this way, the undergrowth evokes an image of the surrounding trees, instead of the conventional pattern where a single bonsai tree would suggest the natural surroundings.

I hope that the variety of plants in this collection will encourage you to expand your concept of bonsai and indeed gardening itself: in a nurturing atmosphere, even something as ordinary as dandelion or bellflower can suddenly take on fresh beauty when planted in just the right way.

I have also included gardening hints for each of the plants in this collection, but you may have to make some adjustments as you work with the bonsai in your climate. Where possible, I have added comments like "this is true for all non-woody plants," and cross-referenced the plant names throughout in the hope that you will be able to experiment further with local varieties of the same plants, and other plants in the same families.

Most of all, I hope that this book will serve as an idea book for bonsai gardeners everywhere. Almost any plant that can be potted is suitable for bonsai; anything that attracts your attention in a garden, in the woods, or by the roadside deserves a chance to be tended in your bonsai nursery. After all, what is more rewarding than the successful cultivation of an entirely new type of bonsai? If you keep experimenting with everything you find—even with the wildflowers that appear in your nursery uninvited—you will ultimately create a garden of bonsai that is fresh, appealing, and truly your own.

Kyuzo Murata
Omiya, Japan

SPRING

Suishi-kaido (a type of Japanese crabapple)

A deciduous shrub or small tree of the Rosaceae.

Suishi-kaido blooms have little resonance, but if you select raw material that is fine-bodied and tractable, it will make a lively and pleasing bonsai. Be sparing with fertilizer and water or it will grow too quickly.

Suishi-kaido (Malus halliana Koehne), mid-April, approx. 70 years, 19 inches (48 cm).

Lily of the valley

A perennial of the Liliaceae.

A simple potted lily of the valley is not very interesting, so remove a clump from its pot and place it in a shallow water basin to make a more distinctive bonsai. The tangled rhizomes will be half-exposed and rise higher each year, creating a miniature mountain wilderness. However, the lily of the valley lacks the strength to hold the soil firmly together, so maintain its vigor by fertilizing well.

Lily of the valley (*Convallaria majalis* L.), late April, potted 20 years, 10 inches (26 cm). *below*

Moltkia

An evergreen shrub of the Boraginaceae. A European cultivated variety.

With proper care, the moltkia will overflow its pot with dazzling blue flowers. Remember to fertilize regularly and protect from winter freezing.

Moltkia (*Moltkia suffruticosa* Brand.), late April, potted 13 years, 22 inches (55 cm). *right*

Japanese flowering quince

A deciduous shrub of the Rosaceae. The *toyonishiki* (shown) is a cultivated variety.

Young flowering quince trees bear white flowers, while trees over 50 years old bear red flowers. In order to achieve the desired dappled pattern of pink and white blossoms, try pruning some of the red-blossomed branches. A white blossom may grow in place of the trimmed branches. Grafting is always an option, but the resulting artificiality will lower the value of the tree. After flowering, wait until the new shoots have nearly stopped growing, then cut them back two or three times until fall, and you will naturally create fine, interestingly curved branches. For another variety, see page 106.

Japanese flowering quince (*Chaenomeles speciosa* Nakai cv. 'Toyonishiki'), mid-April, approx. 70 years, 19 inches (49 cm). *right*

Japanese flowering quince, mid-April, 21 years from cutting, 6 inches (l4 cm). *below*

Zumi (a type of Japanese crabapple)

A small to large deciduous tree of the Rosaceae.

The *zumi* is also called *mitsuba-kaido*, or "three-leaved crabapple." In young trees which have not yet flowered, the leaves are cleft, usually in three. This is one of the many trees in the rose family which are not self-pollinating. It needs another related tree, such as apple or crabapple, in order to bear fruit. For fall aspect, see page 119.

Zumi (***Malus sieboldii*** Rehd.), late April, approx. 50 years, 20 inches (51 cm). *below*

Chinese quince

A deciduous tree of the Rosaceae.

The Chinese quince has complete flowers which bear fruit, and incomplete flowers with immature pistils, which do not bear fruit. Individual trees will vary, but to increase the number of complete flowers, provide plenty of sunlight and fertilizer, and nature will take care of the rest. For fall aspect, see pages 126–27.

Chinese quince (***Chaenomeles sinensis*** Koehne), late April, approx. 70 years, 30 inches (75 cm). *right*

Virginia willow

A deciduous shrub of the Saxifragaceae.

According to records, the Virginia willow was introduced to Japan around 1878, and is now known best for its fall foliage. Its blossoms are a modest white and its fall foliage is long-lasting, adding a bright touch to the winter garden. Give it light protection, such as keeping it away from wind, during periods of severe cold. Sometimes the pot will require more protection than the plant; if the pot has a rim which covers the soil at any point, wrap the pot in plastic during freezing weather to prevent breakage. This is true for all bonsai that will be kept outside in winter.

Virginia willow (*Itea virgineca* L.), late May, 24 years from cutting, 17 inches (44 cm).

Violet

A perennial of the Violaceae.

A single potted violet is modest and sweet, but sometimes, to one's chagrin, it may simply die off. However, when used in a group planting it propagates furiously and will soon take over, if it is not thinned out from time to time. You do not need to repot bonsai with non-woody plants except to change the container, but if you observe signs of weakness in an older plant, carefully divide the rootstock and fertilize.

Violet (*Viola japonica* Langsd.) with *fuchiso* (page 82), late April, potted 15 years, 5 inches (12 cm).

Nigana ("bitter green")

A perennial of the Compositae.

In Japan, there is no need to plant *nigana* deliberately. If there is some growing wild in the vicinity, it will show up in every pot or planter, and act as if it owns the place. Even so, the sight of its tranquil flowers waving in the spring breeze arouses feelings of nostalgia. If there are any similar wildflowers in your area, try giving them a pot of their own; they may surprise you. Just thin the plant out after it flowers to keep it from becoming too much of a pest.

Nigana (*Ixeris dentata* Nakai), mid-May, potted 9 years, 11 inches (27 cm). *below*

Fothergilla

A deciduous shrub of the Hamamelidaceae.

This flowering shrub, imported from North America, is still rare in Japan, but its distinctive brush-shaped flowers have a unique appeal. Its generic name comes from that of the famous British physician and botanist John Fothergill (1712–80).

Fothergilla (*Fothergilla gardenii* Murr.), 10 years, 24 inches (62 cm). *right*

Yamadori-shida (a type of osmunda)

A deciduous fern of the Osmundaceae.

If you dig up a mature clump of this fern and place the rootball in a shallow water basin, you will not need to worry about it drying out. Spread a layer of coarse sand around the clump to hold it in place; there is no need for new soil. When fertilizing, soak well with a weak solution of liquid fertilizer. If the base of the rootstock is up out of the water, there will be no danger of the roots rotting in the dish.

Yamadori-shida (*Osmunda cinnamomea* Pr. var. *fokiensis* Copel), early March, 11 years from collection, 16 inches (40 cm). *below*

Yamadori-shida, early May. *right*

Creeping saxifrage

A perennial of the Saxifragaceae.

Although it is a relative of the highly prized *daimonjiso*, the creeping saxifrage hardly attracts any attention in Japanese bonsai. But if we look at it without preconceptions, we cannot ignore the charm of its lively clusters of flowers. After flowering, it sends out tendrils which must be picked off.

Creeping saxifrage (*Saxifraga stolonifera* Meerb.), mid-June, potted 7 years, 9 inches (23 cm). *below*

Skullcap

A perennial of the Labiatae.

A single skullcap plant is fine, but a clump diverted to one side of the pot is also appealing. The leaves will remain through the winter; trimming is not required, but if you want to let new side shoots grow around the base of the plant, then cut out the old stems.

Skullcap (*Scutellaria indica* var. *parvifolia* Makino form. *alba* Hara), early May, potted 7 years, 2 inches (6 cm). *above*

Skullcap (*Scutellaria indica* var. *parvifolia* Makino), early May, potted 13 years, 2 inches (6 cm). *right*

Field horsetail

A perennial of the Equisetaceae.

Using horsetail for bonsai is difficult, as the dormant rootstocks must be dug up each year. However, when arranged well in a pleasing pot, they can create a miniature aura of springtime. Moss is best arranged once the heads have emerged.

Field horsetail (*Equisetum palustre* L.), mid-April, 2 inches (6 cm). *right*

Mountain ash

A deciduous shrub of the Rosaceae.

In plains areas with long summers, the leaves of the mountain ash receive considerable damage, and one cannot expect fall foliage. However, this is no obstacle to the tree's development. Its growth is slow and differences in age are hard to discern, but the dignity of years will accrue in the end.

Mountain ash (*Sorbus matsumurana* Koehne), late April, approx. 45 years, 21 inches (53 cm). *below*

Spirea

A deciduous shrub of the Rosaceae.

Usually a feeling of age is valued in large bonsai, but the spirea has a tendency to become so tangled its shape is completely lost. It must be continually renewed by pruning out old branches.

Spirea (*Spiraea thunbergii* Sieb.), mid-April, potted approx. 40 years, 17 inches (42 cm). *above*

Cottage pink

A perennial of the Caryophyllaceae.

The flower stalks of the cottage pink stand straight and firm among closely spaced silvery leaves. Because its growth is so dense, you would be wise to take precautions against rot during hot, humid weather.

Cottage pink (*Dianthus plumarius* L.), early June, potted 4 years, 8 inches (21 cm). *right*

Pussywillow

A deciduous shrub of the Salicaceae. The *kuro-yanagi* ("black willow") is a cultivated variety.

Pussywillow cuttings can be started reliably either by letting roots form in water and then planting, or by planting in a cutting bed and keeping the bottom moist. Do not prune immediately after flowering. From May on is optimal, before the shoots grow too long. The contrasting shades of flower "fur" vary, but those of this variety are outstanding.

Kuro-yanagi pussywillow (**Salix gracilistyla** Miq. var. **melanostachys** C. K. Schneider) with *kogumazasa* (*Sasa albo-marginata* Makino et Shibata), mid-April, 23 years from cutting, 5 inches (12 cm).

Forsythia

A deciduous shrub of the Oleaceae.

This variety of the dwarf forsythia has a profusion of flowers that is particularly suited to casual group plantings. Just arrange cuttings in the container you use for propagation, and once they have taken root, move the whole group together into a shallow bonsai dish. When it becomes rootbound, you can remove it from the dish and let the clump grow as it is, and you will never have to repot it again.

Shina forsythia (*Forsythia viridissima* Lindl.), late March, 20 years from cutting, 10 inches (26 cm).

Japanese maple

A deciduous shrub or tree of the Aceraceae. *Seigen*, *deshojo*, and *chizome* are horticultural varieties of the *iroha-momiji*.

The most famous variety, *seigen* (right), is without compare for the brilliant intensity of its new leaf shoots, and has been known as *akaji-nishiki*, or "red brocade," since the sixteenth century. The recently created *deshojo* (below) has some difficulties with leaf color and shape, besides being rather inelegant, but it is fast-growing and easy to propagate. The *chizome* (following page) is a fine, old variety like the *seigen*, and is well loved for its restrained grace despite its pale, weak-looking new shoots. All varieties require very little attention. Just be sure to fertilize well and give them plenty of sun in the early spring in order to make the colors vibrant.

Deshojo maple (*Acer palmatum* Thunb. cv. 'Deshojo'), mid-April, approx. 20 years, 27 inches (68 cm). *below*

Seigen maple (*Acer palmatum* Thunb. form. *seigen* Hort.), mid-April, 50 years from graft, 22 inches (56 cm). *right*

Japanese maple

Chizome maple (*Acer palmatum* Thunb. cv. 'Chizome'), mid-May, 70 years,
52 inches (77 cm).

Japanese andromeda

A deciduous shrub or small tree of the Theaceae. *Akabana-asebi* ("pink-flowered andromeda") is a cultivated variety.

This andromeda is hardy and flowers abundantly. Even a small cutting in a tiny pot will grow lovely blossoms. Fertilize generously, and water sparingly. The andromeda has a long flowering period, so do not hesitate to pick off old flowers and prune at the same time.

Akabana andromeda (***Pieris japonica*** D. Don cv. 'Christmas Cheer'), mid-March, 35 years, 26 inches (65 cm).

Japanese Judas tree

A deciduous tree of the Cercidiphyllaceae.

The Judas tree is well known in Japan as the raw material for fine woodwork. Watching it close at hand, through the passing seasons one catches glimpses of life's poignancy. The Japanese Judas tree can be grown easily from seedlings or cuttings and is excellent for densely planted groupings.

Japanese Judas tree (*Cercidiphyllum japonicum* Sieb. et Zucc.), early June, approx. 15 years, 29 inches (73 cm). *below*

Japanese honeysuckle

A deciduous shrub of the Caprifoliaceae.

The Japanese honeysuckle continually sends out many adventitious shoots from its base, nodes, and so forth, so you must simply keep nipping them off. If you persist in this task, the small, flexible branches will shape the tree naturally for you.

Japanese honeysuckle (*Lonicera gracilipes* Miq. var. *glabra* Miq.), mid-May, approx. 25 years, 15 inches (37 cm). *right*

Dwarf rhododendron

An evergreen shrub of the Theaceae.

The variety shown here, indigenous to Yakushima Island in Kyushu, is superior to other rhododendron varieties for bonsai purposes because it is easy to grow and branches well. However, since it is a high-altitude shrub it does require extra attention, especially during hot summers.

Dwarf rhododendron (*Rhododendron metternichii* Sieb. et Zucc. var. *yakushimanum* Ohwi), mid-May, approx. 45 years, 16 inches (40 cm). *below*

Japanese cherry

A deciduous tree or shrub of the Rosaceae.

The cherry is commonly believed to be one of the more difficult types of bonsai, but the truth is, except for certain varieties, it is extremely strong, long-lived, and easy to cultivate. Fertilize generously, repot yearly, and prune new shoots promptly after flowering, leaving two or three nodes.

Sato cherry (*Prunus lannesiana* Wils. cv. 'Superba'), mid-April, 60 years from graft, 24 inches (60 cm). *right*

Choji cherry (*Prunus apetala* Franch. et Savat.), late February, estimated age over 100 years, 20 inches (50 cm). *following page*

Bald cypress

A deciduous tree of the Cryptomeriaceae.

The wayward branches of the bald cypress are unmanageable, but the delicate grace of the new green foliage more than compensates for the awkwardness. In the spring new shoots will even grow out of the trunk, so prune freely.

Bald cypress (*Taxodium distichum* Rich.), late April, approx. 70 years, 28 inches (70 cm). *right*

Japanese wisteria

A deciduous woody vine of the Leguminosae.

If you allow Japanese wisteria to grow freely in a large pot, it will produce lush vines with few flowers, so be sure to confine it to a small pot.

Japanese wisteria (*Wisteria floribunda* DC.), late April, approx. 70 years, 20 inches (50 cm). *right*

Japanese wisteria buds, mid-April. *top left*

Japanese wisteria pods, early August. *bottom left*

Dwarf azalea

An evergreen shrub of the Theaceae.

This azalea is found in mountainous areas, though it does not grow as high up as the dwarf rhododendron. It is a very difficult task to get it to live longer than about 20 or 30 years, so just keep starting new cuttings to raise a succession of new plants instead.

Dwarf azalea (*Rhododendron kiusianum* Makino) with Siebold's beech (page 90), late April, 25 years from cutting, 10 inches (25 cm).

Silver fir

An evergreen tree of the Pinaceae.

The silver fir is said to grow in boggy areas of the Kurile Islands, but in the Tokyo area we give it only moderate amounts of water. When a living thing is to be cultivated in an unfamiliar environment, we usually try to simulate the plant's native environment as much as possible, but the silver fir does not actually absorb the water of the marshy areas it grows in. We must be sure to pay attention to the actual nature of the plant rather than simply reproducing the superficial qualities of its natural habitat.

Silver fir (*Picea glehnii* Mast.) with skullcap (page 65), late April, 35 years from collection, 12 inches (30 cm). *above*

Silver fir, late April, estimated age over 180 years, 39 inches (100 cm). *following page*

SUMMER

Tomentosa cherry

A deciduous shrub of the Rosaceae. Native to northern China.

Rather than forcing the Tomentosa cherry into a particular form contrary to its nature, let its branches grow and crisscross as they will. Give it plenty of sunlight and fertilizer. It takes up water slowly, so be careful not to let it become waterlogged in the summer.

Tomentosa cherry (*Prunus tomentosa* Thunb.), late May, 35 years, 14 inches (36 cm). *right*

Tomentosa cherry, late March. *below*

Sweet briar

A deciduous shrub of the Rosaceae.

Too much fertilizer will result in thick stems and over-lush foliage, but too little fertilizer will cause severe wilting. It is difficult to achieve just the right balance. The sweet briar requires cross-pollinization, so you will need two plants for it to bear fruit.

Sweet briar (*Rosa rugosa* Thunb.), mid-May, 17 years, 8 inches (20 cm).

Shichidanka (a type of hydrangea)

A deciduous shrub of the Saxifragaceae.

In classical literature the *shichidanka* is associated with the world of dreams, and as bonsai it is a dream come true, because it requires almost no special care. Simply give it light protection in the winter; for the rest, just sit back and let it bloom.

Shichidanka (**Hydrangea macrophylla** Ser. var. *acuminata* Makino form. *prolifera* Nakai), mid-June, 6 years from cutting, 14 inches (36 cm).

Japanese carpinus

A deciduous tree of the Betulaceae.

The Japanese carpinus produces its unusual seed heads every year, but if you break open a husk it will most likely be empty. You can rarely harvest ripe seeds. This would seem the obvious result of the long gap between the flowering times of the male and female flowers. For fall aspect, see pages 116–17.

Japanese carpinus (*Carpinus japonica* Blume), mid-May, 80 years, 28 inches (72 cm).

Hinauchiwa-kaede (a type of maple)

A deciduous tree of the Aceraceae.

This maple does not tolerate strong sunlight, so keep it in the shade during the summer heat. There are not very many examples in circulation, but there is no maple that conveys so well the mystical feeling of spring foliage in a mountain glade. For fall aspect, see page 101.

Hinauchiwa-kaede (***Acer tenuifolium*** Koidz.), early May, estimated age over 70 years, 28 inches (72 cm).

Ladies' tresses

A perennial of the Orchidaceae.

This wildflower crops up anywhere and insists on being noticed. It is difficult to grow alone, but when planted with a grass it is undaunted by moisture or dryness, heat or cold.

Ladies' tresses (**Spiranthes sinensis** var. **amoena** Hara) with **himei** (**Juncus effusus** L. form. **gracilis** Buch.), early July, 8 inches (21 cm). *below*

Ladies' tresses with broad-leaved plantain (**Plantago asiatica**) and skullcap (page 29), early July, 7 inches (17 cm). *right*

Oleaster

A deciduous shrub of the Elaeagnaceae.

Like the Chinese quince (see pages 21 and 126), the oleaster has many flowers which do not produce fruit, so give it plenty of sunlight and fertilizer. If you let adventitious shoots grow, the trunk will swell where they come out. This is not only unsightly but may fatally injure the tree, so do not neglect pruning.

Oleaster (*Eleagnus multiflora* Thunb. var. *hortensis* Serv. cv. 'Gigantea'), mid-June, 39 years from cutting, 7 inches (19 cm).

Hitotsubatago (a type of fringe tree)

A deciduous tree of the Oleaceae.

In the early summer this tree is crowned with a cloud of white blossoms. Until 1931, a famous old *hitotsubatago*, designated a Natural Monument, stood at an intersection of six streets in the Aoyama district of Tokyo, in an area that is now part of the outer garden of the Meiji Shrine. Even today the *hitotsubatago* is sometimes referred to as *rokudo-boku*, "the tree of six streets."

Hitotsubatago (*Chionanthus retusus* Lindl. et Paxt.), mid-May, estimated age over 120 years, 35 inches (90 cm). *far right*

Hitotsubatago fruit, early October. *right*

Hitotsubatago, early May, estimated age over 120 years, 33 inches (85 cm). *below*

Cherokee rose

An evergreen climbing shrub of the Rosaceae.

When I am overwhelmed with improved varieties, I find fresh pleasure in returning to the simplicity and gentleness of the original Cherokee rose. Among the varieties is one which has pale pink blooms. Carefully nip off adventitious shoots and grow in a sunny place.

Cherokee rose (*Rosa laevigata* Michx.), mid-May, 60 years, 22 inches (55 cm).

Japanese honeysuckle

An evergreen or semideciduous climbing shrub of the Caprifoliaceae.

What country child has not sipped the drop of sweet nectar from the base of a honeysuckle flower? This variety is quieter than the one shown on page 39, but both are lovely. In the wild the vine grows indefinitely, but when potted it can be trained into a fine trunk.

Japanese honeysuckle (*Lonicera japonica* Thunb.), late May, approx. 50 years, 24 inches (60 cm). *below*

Japanese honeysuckle fruit, mid-November. *right*

Kusayoshi

A perennial of the Graminaceae. The *shima-kusayoshi* has white-striped leaves.

This is a wild grass of the seashore. When you collect *kusayoshi*, you can dig up a clump, or simply take cuttings. The cuttings will easily take root if snipped off at a node, and once planted, the stalks will come up year after year. This simple grass exquisitely expresses the essence of not only summer, but each season in turn.

Shima-kusayoshi (Phalaris arundinacea L. var. picta L.), early June, potted 7 years, 16 inches (40 cm). *left*

Kusayoshi (Phalaris arundinacea L.), late June, potted 12 years, 20 inches (50 cm). *right*

Quaking grass

An annual of the Graminaceae. Native to Europe.

If you sow quaking grass in the spring in a large clump, it will end up looking like a weed, so plant it late and fertilize sparingly. Experienced bonsai gardeners may prefer to keep a respectful distance from annuals like this one. It is indeed troublesome to have to plant it every year, but it does such a fine job of portraying a world of subtle and profound elegance that it is hard to resist its strange power.

Quaking grass (*Briza maxima* L.), early June, 7 inches (17 cm). *left*
Quaking grass, mid-June, 8 inches (20 cm). *right*

Water lily

A perennial of the Nymphaeceae. Cultivated variety.

To enjoy this miniature water lily in a small dish, divide it each year
and put each shoot in a new dish. The water should not be so deep
that the sun cannot reach the rootstock. To fertilize, just put a piece
of dried fish or a pellet of organic fertilizer in at the edge of the dish.
The fish will neither cloud the water nor smell bad.

Water lily (*Nymphaea tetragona* Georgi var. *helvora* Hort.), mid-August.

Shotaiso (a type of sedge)

A perennial of the Cyperaceae.

Once summer is past, the leaves of the *shotaiso* grow sloppily, and the dead leaves are unsightly. If you cut it back once before it reaches that stage, you will be able to enjoy it through the fall as well. Cut back old growth at the base before the new shoots begin to grow. Growing a single seedling in a small pot can be fascinating also. Although many grasses resemble the *shotaiso*, none is quite like it.

Shotaiso (*Carex sp.*), early June, potted 7 years, 7 inches (18 cm). *below*

Shotaiso flowers, early March. *left*

Sheep sorrel

An annual or biennial of the Polygonaceae. Native to Eurasia.

Unlike most naturalized plants, the sheep sorrel has something very Japanese about it. Its reddish flower heads swaying in the May breeze are especially suggestive. Even in the winter it can be appealing. Give it plenty of sunlight, but not too much water or fertilizer. After flowering is over, cut it back completely.

Sheep sorrel (*Rumex acetosella* L.) with Chinese bellflower (*Platycodon grandiflorum*) and Nyoi violet (*Viola verecunda* A. Gray), early June, potted 30 years, 6 inches (16 cm).

Self-heal

A perennial of the Labiatae.

Self-heal, so called because it was originally thought to have medicinal properties, tends to look a little uncontrolled if grown by itself. As always, though, the added effect of a member of the rice family is amazing. Here I have used *chikara-shiba*, a Japanese wild grass, in the supporting role, but anything that will fill in the spaces between the stalks is fine. After flowering is over, keep the arrangement neat by removing any shoots that extend out too far.

Self-heal (*Prunella vulgaris* var. *lilacina*) with *chikara-shiba* (*Pennisetum alopecuroides*), mid-June, potted 5 years, 10 inches (26 cm).

Crape myrtle

A deciduous tree of the Lythraceae.

Even more than the silk tree (see page 94), the crape myrtle likes a continental climate and will not flower in a cool summer. The crape myrtle is especially vulnerable to parasites like plant lice and scale insects, which cause unsightly black spot disease. They must be controlled with pesticides for any hope of a perfect bonsai.

Crape myrtle (*Lagerstroemia indica* L.), late August, approx. 60 years, 35 inches (90 cm). *below*

Japanese hemlock

An evergreen tree of the Pinaceae.

Most evergreen bonsai show little change over the seasons, but the new shoots of the Ezo pine and the Japanese hemlock are superb, no less thrilling than the blossoms of other trees. Nip off all the spring shoots and let the summer shoots grow. If you leave even a few spring shoots, the needles will be disordered and unsightly, so nip them off completely, and double the ordinary amount of fertilizer in springtime.

Japanese hemlock (*Tsuga sieboldii* Carr.), early June, estimated age over 90 years, 29 inches (73 cm). *right*

Spruce

An evergreen tree of the Pinaceae.

The spruce is uncommon in Japanese bonsai but has become a favorite among American bonsai gardeners, both because of its awe-inspiring form and the ready availability of raw material. New shoots will only appear on the tips of the branches. In order to shorten a branch, twist the bud off before it opens, and a new bud may appear in the middle of the branch. If it does, cut off the rest of the branch beyond the point where the new bud appears.

Spruce (*Picea polita* Carr.), late May, estimated age over 120 years, 33 inches (85 cm). *left*

Orange

An evergreen shrub of the Rutaceae.

Even in a small pot, all flowers will bear fruit, and the branches are easy to train. Citrus trees require a great deal of fertilizer: otherwise, the leaves turn yellow and lose vigor, and, like the Chinese quince (see pages 21 and 126), the flowers will stop bearing fruit. This tree is winter-hardy and will even withstand light frost.

Orange (*Citrus sp.*), mid-May, approx. 50 years, 22 inches (57 cm). *below*

Orange flowers, mid-May. *right*

Stewartia

A deciduous tree of the Theaceae.

Stewartia trees have considerable individual variation in the way blossoms are attached to the stems. If you want to enjoy high-quality flowers, you must select good raw material—preferably cuttings taken from parent trees that bear plenty of flowers. The stewartia's sturdiness, however, belying the ephemeral beauty of its flowers, makes it a champion among trees.

Stewartia (*Stewartia pseudo-camellia* Maxim.), mid-June, 28 years from cutting, 29 inches (73 cm).

Himeshara (a type of stewartia)

A deciduous tree of the Theaceae.

For a group planting of *himeshara* you must first be sure you have material with pliable roots. If you cannot find such specimens, you will have to grow them yourself. Fortunately, the *himeshara* is easy to grow from seed or cuttings. It does not overwinter well, so shallow pots must be protected.

Himeshara (*Stewartia monadelpha* Sieb. et Zucc.), mid-June, 25 years, 24 inches (62 cm). *below*

Himeshara flowers, mid-June. *right*

Gold-banded lily

A perennial of the Liliaceae.

These lily blossoms will not stay on for more than two weeks, but the plant can be enjoyed for a while by planting bulbs or seed in a clump of grass. Either eulalia or *fuchiso* will allow it to grow without any difficulty.

Gold-banded lily (*Lilium auratum* Lindl.) with *fuchiso* (page 82), early August, potted 16 years, 24 inches (60 cm).

Tama-ajisai (a type of hydrangea)

A deciduous shrub of the Saxifragaceae.

Usually it takes many years of perseverance to train a plant collected from the wild, but the *tama-ajisai* is an exception. It becomes a mature and pleasing bonsai by the second year. The suspense of waiting for its large, tight buds to burst open is delicious.

Tama-ajisai (Hydrangea involucrata Sieb.), early July, 8 years, 11 inches (29 cm).

Sakko-fuji (a type of wisteria)

An evergreen woody vine of the Leguminosae.

There is considerable individual variation in this wisteria, so if you do not select a young tree with short spaces between nodes and many branches, you will be sorry later. Regrettably, the small, elegant *satsuma* variety (right) is difficult to propagate. At any rate, since the flowers form at the tips of the new shoots, let them grow without pruning.

Hosoba-sakko-fuji (*Millettia reticulata* Benth. var. *stenophylla* Merr. et Chun), late August, approx. 80 years, total length 40 inches (100 cm). *below*

Satsuma-sakko-fuji (*Millettia reticulata* Benth. cv. 'Satsumasakkofuji'), mid-August, 15 years from graft, 15 inches (37 cm). *right*

Scouring rush

An evergreen perennial of the Equisetaceae.

This reed requires generous amounts of water, and does well in a water basin. Use coarse sand in the basin rather than soil to stabilize the roots. Water horsetail is a more delicate variety that dies down above the soil in the winter, but the roots remain. Handle it in the same way as you would scouring rush.

Scouring rush (*Equisetum hyemale* L.), late June, potted 2 years, 18 inches (46 cm). *below left*

Water horsetail (*Equisetum fluviatile* L.), mid-June, potted 2 years, 9 inches (24 cm). *below right*

Taiwan-ogi ("Taiwan reed")

A perennial of the Graminaceae.

Place this plant out of direct sunlight and remove old stems and leaves whenever necessary to create a cool, refreshing atmosphere. To propagate, take cuttings of new shoots close to the soil surface and put them in water as you would willow cuttings. Fertilize them once they have rooted and they will grow quickly. If the plant gets too much sun, the shoots will become fine and dense without growing longer, and you will have to start over again with fresh cuttings.

Taiwan-ogi (*Arundo formosana* Hack.), early July, potted 20 years, total length 53 inches (135 cm). *right*

Blue flag

A perennial of the Iridaceae.

The blue flag flowers poorly in the shade, so give it plenty of sunlight and fertilizer. It is not necessary to divide the clump when repotting.

Blue flag (*Iris sanguinea* Hornem), mid-May, potted 7 years, 13 inches (33 cm). *below*

Blue flag flowers, mid-May. *left*

Terihano-ibara (a type of wild rose)

A deciduous shrub of the Rosaceae.

The *terihano-ibara* is managed differently from other wild roses, in that all new shoots from the base are removed, leaving only the old trunks. This rose needs cross-pollination. If there are wild roses in the vicinity, bees will pollinate it, but if not you must provide at least one other plant and cross-pollinate them manually.

Terihano-ibara (**Rosa wichuraiana** Crep.), mid-October, 30 years, 7 inches (17 cm).

Bellflower

A perennial of the Campanulaceae.

The bellflower just will not stay in one place. It scatters its seeds far and wide, giving us the pleasure of meeting it again in some unexpected pot. It is never in the way, wherever it appears.

Bellflower (*Campanula punctata* Lam.), mid-June, potted 16 years, 9 inches (24 cm). *below*

Bellflower with *nokongiku* (page 131), early July, potted 8 years, 7 inches (19 cm). *right*

Amacha (a type of hydrangea)

A deciduous shrub of the Saxifragaceae.

The miniature flowers of this small shrub are long-lasting. It does not have the lush vigor of most wild plants, but it makes an interesting addition to a bonsai collection. Do not forget to prune adventitious shoots repeatedly.

Amacha (**Hydrangea macrophylla** Ser. var. *thunbergii* Makino), mid-June, 9 years from cutting, 12 inches (30 cm).

Pomegranate

A deciduous tree of the Punicaceae. The white-flowered variety pictured is a cultivated one.

The pomegranate likes a dry climate and will drop leaves during prolonged rainy periods, although this does not damage the tree itself. As long as it has fertilizer it is a good-natured glutton and easy to manage. This double-petaled variety bears lovely flowers but no fruit; if you prefer growing the fruit, then select a single-petaled variety.

Pomegranate (**Punica granatum** L. form. *multiplex* Sweet), mid-June, 45 years, 12 inches (30 cm).

Siebold's beech

A deciduous tree of the Fagaceae.

After new shoots have stopped growing, nip off the undesirable ones, selecting according to direction and length of nodes. If the shoots continue to grow after pruning, the tree has been getting too much fertilizer, so reduce accordingly. Leaves are easily damaged by lack of water or direct summer sunlight, but this does not endanger the tree itself.

Siebold's beech (*Fagus crenata* Blume), mid-May, approx. 45 years, 29 inches (73 cm). *below*

Siebold's beech, mid-February. *upper right*

Siebold's beech, early November. *lower right*

Natsu-fuji ("summer wisteria")

A deciduous woody vine of the Leguminosae.

In contrast to the spring-blooming wisteria, the *natsu-fuji* has trim, simple racemes that are cool and refreshing in the summer months. The tree is easy to grow from cuttings. If you grow it in a small pot and keep it small, you can appreciate its flowers more fully. In cold areas it will need winter protection.

Natsu-fuji (Millettia japonica A. Gray), early July, approx. 70 years, 18 inches (46 cm).

Weeping willow

A deciduous tree of the Salicaeae.

The branches of the weeping willow will not droop naturally when the plant is potted, so you must train the new twigs by bending them down at strategic points by hand. Prune branches back to their base every spring, and repot once a year.

Weeping willow (*Salix babylonica* L.), early July, 17 years from cutting, total length 28 inches (70 cm).

Silk tree

A deciduous tree of the Leguminaceae.

In the haiku poet Basho's travel diary *The Narrow Road to the Deep North*, the silk tree is described as being lovely when its flowers are misty with rain. Actually, after a rain the flower filaments are ruined, losing their color and becoming quite miserable-looking. This tree is a true child of the sun and is not happy unless the weather is so swelteringly hot that we humans are absolutely helpless.

Silk tree (*Albizza julibrissin* Durazz.), late June, approx. 25 years, 25 inches (64 cm). *below*

Silk tree flowers, late June. *right*

Japanese hawthorn

A deciduous shrub of the Rosaceae.

This tree's flowers are easily pollinated by a tree of another family, and one tree alone will have difficulty bearing fruit, so place two hawthorns from different parents next to each other. If you use too much fertilizer, the fruit will darken and drop off, so keep the fertilizer level slightly lower than that of other fruit-bearing bonsai. The red-flowered hawthorn, native to Europe and northern Africa, is hardier than this Japanese variety.

Japanese hawthorn (*Crataegus cuneata* Sieb. et Zucc.), mid-September, approx. 35 years, 20 inches (52 cm). *below*

Japanese hawthorn, mid-May. *right*

Yamakobashi

A deciduous shrub of the Lauraceae.

The *yamakobashi* has the characteristic camphor smell of the laurel family. It is easy to recognize in the woods because it holds its withered leaves into the winter. You are fortunate if you can find wild seedlings, because nothing is better for starting a group planting.

Yamakobashi (**Lindera glauca** Blume), early November, approx. 39 years, 22 inches (56 cm).

Trident maple

A deciduous tree or shrub of the Aceraceae.

To enjoy the fall foliage of trident maple, you must keep the leaves from being damaged or aging prematurely. Move the tree into the shade during hot summer weather to prevent leaf-burn, and return it to a sunny spot when summer is over. Trim off the leaves as you see fit; the tree will not be damaged. After that, just hope for good autumn weather.

Trident maple (*Acer buergerianum* **Mig.**), early November, approx. 50 years, 19 inches (48 cm). *below*

Hinauchiwa-kaede (another type of maple; *Acer tenuifolium* **Koidz.**), early November, estimated age over 80 years, 35 inches (90 cm). See also page 55. *right*

Japanese maple

A deciduous tree of the Aceraceae.

The Japanese maple requires very little water (only slightly more than the pines), so keep your maples on the dry side. Excess water will not harm them internally, but makes the roots grow up through the soil surface in an unsightly way.

Iroha maple (*Acer palmatum* Thunb.), early November, approx. 35 years, 22 inches (55 cm). *right*

Yatsubusa maple (*Acer palmatum* Thunb. cv. 'Yatsubusa'), mid-November, approx. 40 years, 18 inches (46 cm). *below*

Narrowleaf firethorn

An evergreen shrub of the Rosaceae.

Many fall fruit-bearing bonsai have troublesome idiosyncrasies, such as being unisexual or requiring cross-pollinization, but as long as this shrub, which thrives in any climate, bears flowers it is sure to bear fruit. Also, nipping off the shoots will not damage the shrub itself, so the perfect shape can be attained easily.

Narrowleaf firethorn (*Pyracantha angustifolia* Schneid.), late September, approx. 40 years, 18 inches (46 cm). *below*

Narrowleaf firethorn, mid-May. *right*

Ivy

An evergreen woody vine of the Araliaceae.

Vines climb by means of aerial roots which may grow as long as ten yards. However, when potted, ivy sheds all traces of its former climbing nature. The majority of other woody vines also flower and fruit abundantly as bonsai.

Ivy (*Hedera rhombea* Sieb. et Zucc.), late September, approx. 70 years, 22 inches (56 cm).

Japanese flowering quince

A deciduous shrub of the Rosacea. *Chojubai* (shown) is a horticultural variety.

This variety is said to grow wild on the Japan Sea side of western Japan. It has large-leaved, small-leaved, white-flowered, and year-round flowering varieties, among others. Propagation is from cuttings. Cut a rhizome into pieces, arrange the pieces in a pot, and cover them with soil. They will send up shoots everywhere and branch out generously, creating a group planting which transcends technique. For another variety of flowering quince, see page 18.

Japanese flowering quince (*Chaenomeles japonica* Lindl. cv. 'Chojubai'), late June, 30 years from cutting, 13 inches (33 cm). *bottom*

Japanese flowering quince, late March. *top*

Japanese toad lily

A perennial of the Liliaceae.

No matter how hard you try, you cannot keep the toad lily for long. It will disappear in a few years. But that is its nature and cannot be helped. The variety shown at right should be repotted yearly, moved into the shade during the summer, and given water and fertilizer regularly.

Kii-joro toad lily (***Tricyrtis macranthopsis*** Masamune), early October, total length 9 inches (23 cm). *right*

Kibananotsuki toad lily (***Tricyrtis perfoliata*** Masamune), mid-October, total length 13 inches (33 cm). *below*

Tsurusoba (a type of knotweed)

A perennial of the Polygonaceae.

This plant cannot endure cold, so keep it indoors through the winter. If you cut it back after it blooms in the spring and let the new shoots grow, it will bloom again in early summer. After that you can cut back the long stems and wait for it to bloom once more in the fall. You may raise plants from seed every spring, but they will not match plants made from cuttings of older plants.

Tsurusoba (Persicaria chinensis Nakai) with *akabana* (*Epilobium phyrricholophum* Franch. et Savat.), early November, potted 5 years, 6 inches (15 cm). *below*

Wild grape

A deciduous woody vine of the Vitaceae.

Fruit from early flowers will have an uninteresting dirty white color, so cut back vines around June and let the new shoots grow. From a later flowering you will be able to enjoy the multicolored beads of fall fruit. Whether collected from the wild or grown from a cutting, the wild grape will bear fruit in the same year.

Wild grape (*Ampelopsis brevipedunculata* Trautv.), mid-October, potted 13 years, total length 28 inches (70 cm). *right*

Inu-biwa (a type of fig)

A deciduous shrub of the Moraceae.

Rather than taking the time and trouble to make a large bonsai of this fig, simply grow it from a cutting in a small pot. It will be easy to handle, appealing, and pleasant.

Inu-biwa (Ficus erecta Thunb.), mid-June, 7 years from cutting, **6 inches (14 cm)**. *right*

Red chokeberry

A deciduous shrub of the Rosaceae.

The chokeberry is uncommon in Japanese bonsai, but it bears fruit reliably every year, and is hardy and easy to grow. Its trunks do not thicken at all, but its rhizomes will send up shoots everywhere, creating a natural group planting.

Red chokeberry (Aronia arbutifolia L.), mid-October, approx. **30 years, 33 inches (83 cm)**. *below*

Welsh onion flower

A perennial of the Liliaceae.

This is not a plant associated with water, but it is well suited to being grown on a rock, or removed from its pot and placed in a shallow water basin.

Welsh onion flower (*Hosta sp.*), mid-September, potted 14 years, 7 inches (18 cm). *right*

Iwashajin (a type of ladybells)

A perennial of the Campanulaceae.

Treat this plant like the Japanese toad lily (page 107) and leave the rest to the weather. In a long, hot spell its leaves will wither and it will hardly flower. Even so, it is basically hardy and will send out vigorous shoots in the spring, so you must be untiringly patient with it.

Iwashajin (*Adenophora takedae* Makino), mid-September, total length 15 inches (39 cm). *below*

Tea bush

An evergreen shrub of the Theaceae.

The tea bush is far from the level of elegant simplicity desired in a bonsai, but a group planting like this one will grow lively blossoms. Cuttings will begin to flower in two to three years and even seedlings will flower in several years. After that it is a matter of waiting for the planting to mature year by year. Fertilize generously and water sparingly.

Tea bush (*Camellia sinensis* O. Kuntze), early October, approx. 40 years from seed, 17 inches (44 cm). *below*

Japanese linden

A deciduous tree of the Tiliaceae.

Besides the pines, there are many trees that are believed to have a symbiotic mycorrhizal relationship with certain fungi. During rainy periods the white hyphae climb up this linden, sometimes even enveloping the trunk. In the fall, rows of tiny mushrooms add a pleasant element of surprise to your bonsai.

Japanese linden (*Tilia japonica* Simonkai), late September, approx. 60 years, 35 inches (88 cm). *right*

Ginkgo

A deciduous tree of the Ginkgoaceae.

Grown naturally, the ginkgo matures rapidly and lives for many years, but potted it requires careful management. In particular do not neglect feeding. If the ginkgo does not get plenty of sunlight and fertilizer, the leaves will not grow thick and you will not get good yellow fall foliage. Scars will not heal, so avoid cutting large branches.

Ginkgo (*Ginkgo biloba* L.), mid-October, approx. 70 years, 26 inches (65 cm). *left*

Japanese hornbeam

A deciduous tree of the Betulaceae.

As the Japanese hornbeam ages, branches die, and it becomes very difficult to manage. When the odd weak branch dies, it is a physiological phenomenon and cannot be helped, but an extreme number probably reflects malnourishment, so make adjustments in the amount of fertilizer according to the tree's condition.

Japanese hornbeam (*Carpinus laxiflora* Blume), mid-October, approx. 40 years, 24 inches (61 cm). *below*

Japanese carpinus

A deciduous tree of the Betulaceae.

This tree's pollination scheme remains a mystery, and individual trees vary in how well they flower, so select your raw material very carefully. For spring aspect, see page 54.

Japanese carpinus (*Carpinus japonica* Blume), mid-November, approx. 50 years, 24 inches (62 cm). *right*

Japanese carpinus, early July. *below*

117

Sumac

A deciduous tree of the Anacardiaceae.

If you plant sumac seeds in a shallow tray, by fall you will be able to enjoy a tiny forest of colorful foliage. When the trunks become old and overgrown, you may cut them back wherever you wish, and they will send out new shoots. Some people get a rash from contact with sumac sap, so if you have sensitive skin, wear gloves when handling this tree.

Sumac (Rhus succedanea L.), early October, 12 years from seed, 16 inches (41 cm). *below*

Zumi (a type of Japanese crabapple)

A deciduous tree of the Rosaceae.

In the general trend toward pomp and splendor, bonsai with large red berries have become widespread, and the red-berried varieties of Japanese crabapple have become very popular. But the *zumi*'s pale-orange berries make it a fine bonsai redolent with traditional Japanese sentiment. For spring aspect, see page 20.

Zumi (Malus sieboldii Rehd.), mid-November, approx. 50 years, 20 inches (51 cm). *upper right*

Zumi, early October. *lower right*

Japanese zelkova

A deciduous tree of the Ulmaceae.

The zelkova is a typical sun-loving tree. Keep it out of the shade, prune the leaves at least once, and trim the tips of the branches so that sunlight can reach all the way to the inner branches.

Japanese zelkova (*Zelkova serrata* Makino), early September, approx. 80 years, 37 inches (95 cm). *far right*

Japanese zelkova, late January. *right*

Japanese zelkova, late October. *below*

Gonzui

A deciduous tree of the Staphyleaceae.

The *gonzui* grows wild in the woods and regenerates vigorously. Once you have planted a sapling taken from the wild, you will never lack for raw material. Even if you cut off the entire tree at the base, the severed trunk will send up new shoots. When the cutting or sapling has taken root, just cut it back whenever it grows too long, and soon it will bear fruit.

Gonzui (*Euscaphis japonica* Kanitzu), early October, potted approx. 30 years, 21 inches (53 cm). *below*

Gonzui buds, mid-May. *right*

Japanese spindle tree

A deciduous shrub of the Celastraceae.

The spindle tree has long nodes, so it is not amenable to training. The unrestrained branches are what gives it its special character, and if you go against its nature, the result will look artificial. Besides the ordinary pink-fruited variety, lively crimson-fruited and white-fruited varieties are now available.

Japanese spindle tree (*Euonymus sieboldianus* Blume), late October, approx. 45 years, 24 inches (60 cm).

Iigiri

A deciduous tree of the Flacourtiaceae.

The *iigiri* is unisexual, and uncommon either cultivated or wild, so be sure to get trees of both sexes. The
red berries at the ends of the branches in the winter
are a sight not to be missed.

Iigiri (**Idesia polycarpa** Maxim.), mid-October, approx. 20 years
from graft, 21 inches (54 cm). *below*

Binan-kazura ("good-looking-man vine")

An evergreen woody vine of the Schisandraceae.

The *binan-kazura* is completely dependent on wind for
pollination. If there is a wild tree in the vicinity, your
bonsai will bear fruit without difficulty, but if not, you
will have to cross-pollinate it. Male flowers are short-
lived, so pick them early in the morning without scat-
tering the pollen and split them open over the female flowers. The pollen will float down, so give more
to the flowers at the top of the tree.

Binan-kazura artificial pollination, late July. *upper right*

Binan-kazura (**Kadsura japonica** Dunal), early October, approx.
70 years, 20 inches (52 cm). *lower right*

Chinese quince

A deciduous tree of the Rosaceae.

If you wish simply to appreciate the fruit of the Chinese quince, graft a cutting from a tree which bears fruit, and your quince will soon bear fruit of its own. However, for a long-lived tree, you must grow the Chinese quince from seed. For spring aspect, see page 21.

Chinese quince (*Chaenomeles sinensis* Koehne), late November, approx. 60 years, 32 inches (81 cm). *right*

Chinese quince, late November, approx. 20 years from graft, 22 inches (55 cm). *below*

Stauntonia

An evergreen woody vine of the Lardizabalaceae.

The stauntonia is typical of trees which require cross-pollinization; one alone will not amount to anything. Obtain at least two trees, fertilize generously, and water sparingly. Vines which grow too long should be nipped back early, as they have no effect on the flowers. The stauntonia thrives in the shade, and has a modern look similar to indoor foliage plants that is handsome in any setting.

Stauntonia (*Stauntonia hexaphylla* Decne.), early November, approx. 20 years, total length 27 inches (68 cm). *right*

Stauntonia, mid-July. *below*

Broomrape

An annual parasitic plant of the Orobanchaceae.

When you pot this well-known parasitic plant with eulalia as a host, you cannot save the host from declining, no matter how hard you try. Do feed and water the broomrape and eulalia with care; sometimes cutting back the eulalia severely will help it revive. But when the time comes, you must put in new eulalia and grow the broomrape from seed again.

Broomrape (*Aeginetia indica* L.) with eulalia (*Miscanthus sinesis* Anderss. form. *gracillimus* cv. 'Yakushima susuki'), late August, potted 6 years, 4 inches (11 cm).

Nokongiku (a type of aster)

A perennial of the Compositae.

The *nokongiku* prefers soil on the dry side, so avoid overwatering. During its flowering period the pot surface will be rather sparse unless you plant another grass or wildflower with it to dress it up. You may cut back the main stems once and let the side shoots grow, but if you keep it too trim you will lose its autumnal atmosphere.

Nokongiku (*Aster ageratoides* Turcz. var. *ovatus* Nakai) with *mizuhiki* (*Polygonum filiforme* Thunb.) and *kumazasa* (*Sasa albo-marginata* Makino et Shibata), late October, potted 20 years, 10 inches (25 cm).

Japanese ivy

A deciduous woody vine of the Vitaceae.

The ivy vine itself is quite strong, but it can be a struggle to protect the leaves from insect damage and sunburn. Also, if the vine does not get enough fertilizer, the leaves will drop before they change color, so it is not easy to achieve good fall foliage.

Japanese ivy (*Parthenocissus tricuspidata* Planch.), late October, approx. 70 years, total length 20 inches (50 cm). *right*

Japanese ivy, mid-November. *below*

Oregano

A perennial of the Labiatae.

Oregano grows in a clump like its relative the skullcap (see page 29). The fine, pale-purple flowers and evocative, frosty-looking foliage make this familiar herb an ideal candidate for bonsai, and of course the cuttings have a culinary use as well. As anyone who keeps a kitchen garden knows, oregano is easy to grow and resistant to heat, cold, and insect damage.

Oregano (*Origanum vulgare* L.) with cranesbill (*Geranium nepalense* var. *thunbergii*), mid-November, potted 8 years. *below*

Shiraki ("white tree")

A small deciduous tree of the Euphorbiaceae.

The *shiraki* offers many seasonal delights. In the spring the tips of its new buds look like little birds' beaks. And in the fall, its large red leaves have a clear, open brightness. This tree is not winter-hardy and needs protection from wind and frost in cold areas. Its sparse branches are tractable, so all you need to do is prune the shoots.

Shiraki (*Sapium japonicum* Pax.), early November, approx. 30 years, 33 inches (83 cm). *right*

Ko-mayumi (a type of spindle tree)

A deciduous shrub of the Celastraceae.

There are phenomena in nature which baffle the casual observer. As far as we know, the wings on the branches of the winged spindle tree (*nishikigi*) serve no purpose whatsoever and are only a nuisance. The *ko-mayumi* has the same leaves, flowers, and fruit as the winged spindle tree, but lacks the wings, so it is a refreshing and welcome change. In any case, it is easy to care for, requiring water only when the soil dries out.

Ko-mayumi (*Euonymus alatus* Sieb. form. *ciliatodentatus* Hiyama), early November, approx. 50 years, 13 inches (34 cm).

WINTER

Isojansho

An evergreen shrub of the Rosaceae.

The *isojansho*'s clusters of recurved leaves resemble a flock of geese, hence its poetic name "call of the wild geese." In the winter it must be brought indoors, but it does not need a heated room. Take cuttings during midsummer, as they will not root well in cool weather.

Isojansho (**Osteomeles anthyllidifolia** Lindl.), late November, approx. 50 years, total length 20 inches (52 cm). *far right*

Isojansho fruit, late October. *right*

Isojansho, early June. *below*

Tachi-mayumi (a type of spindle tree)

A deciduous shrub of the Celastraceae.

You will not encounter this cultivated variety of the Japanese spindle tree (see page 123) outside the bonsai world. Its colorful foliage brightens the early winter months. However, the leaves will drop soon after the temperature falls, so bring it inside after the first heavy frost in order to enjoy it longer.

Tachi-mayumi (**Euonymus sieboldianus** Blume cv. 'Fastigiatus'), early December, approx. 30 years, 26 inches (66 cm).

Persimmon

A deciduous tree of the Ebenaceae.

The variety shown is the wild predecessor from which cultivated varieties have been developed. This variety (*yamagaki*) is also familiarly known as *saru-nakase*, or "makes-a-monkey-cry," an exaggeration of the fruit's astringency. The persimmon dislikes having its roots dry out, so choose a cloudy, windless day for repotting and do it quickly. Give this tree plenty of water, fertilizer, and sunlight.

Yamagaki persimmon (**Diospyros kaki** Thunb. var. *sylvestris* Makino), early December, potted approx. 45 years, 27 inches (69 cm).

Bamboo

A perennial of the Graminaceae.

The bamboo's rhizomes will coil around in the bottom of the pot and push up the soil, so lift the clump from the pot once a year and prune the rhizomes back. Trim off old leaves every year before the new ones come out.

Kurotake bamboo (***Phyllostachys nigra*** Munro), late October, potted 60 years, 22 inches (55 cm). *far right*

Hobichiku bamboo, early September. *below*

Hoochiku bamboo, mid-September, 6 years, 6 inches (15 cm). *right*

Needle juniper

An evergreen of the Cupressaceae.

The old Japanese name for this tree, *nezumi-sashi*, or "mouse sticker," comes from the tree's folk usage as a rodent repellent because of its sharp needles. It is no exaggeration to say that care of the needle juniper begins and ends with pruning. Prune shoots conscientiously from spring through fall.

Needle juniper (*Juniperus rigida* Sieb. et Zucc.), late March, estimated age over 150 years, 20 inches (50 cm).   *below*

Needle juniper, early December, estimated age over 120 years, 37 inches (94 cm). *right*

Needle juniper

Needle juniper, late March, estimated age over 90 years, total length 18 inches
(45 cm). *below*

Sargent juniper

An evergreen shrub of the Cupressaceae.

The sargent juniper is an exception among bonsai in that it has a highly diffuse, even abstract, form. Natural specimens are rare and difficult to obtain. It is vulnerable to pollution, so build up its defenses by conscientious fertilizing and repotting.

Sargent juniper (*Juniperus chinensis* L. var. *sargentii* Henry), 23 inches (58 cm).

Japanese apricot

A deciduous tree of the Rosaceae.

There is an old saying that the way to get the Japanese apricot to bloom is to let it dry out in the summer and force it to the brink of death. But in my experience, the apricot blooms just fine with ordinary care. If anything, you may have to devise a way to guard against the harmful effects of over-blooming.

Japanese apricot (*Prunus mume* Sieb. et Zucc.), late February, approx. 100 years, 29 inches (74 cm). *right*

Japanese apricot, late February, approx. 60 years, 28 inches (67 cm). *below*

Japanese black pine

An evergreen of the Pinaceae.

To achieve uniform short needles, cut back all new shoots (around early July, depending on location). At the same time prune out any areas where there are too many old needles. Once the old needles are uniform, let the new shoots grow a second time. If you leave too many old needles, the new shoots will not grow in evenly.

Japanese black pine (*Pinus thunbergii* Parl.), early December, approx. 120 years from seedling, 15 inches (37 cm).

Japanese white pine

An evergreen of the Pinaceae.

In a healthy tree, the symbiotic mycorrhizal relationship between pine and fungus is most striking. The hyphae, which look like a white mold, spread throughout the pot and even out the drainage holes. Sometimes the fungus is visible on the soil surface, but not at other times, such as when this picture was taken. If you are not satisfied with a tree's condition, try transplanting hyphae from another tree.

Japanese white pine (*Pinus parviflora* Sieb. et Zucc.), late March, estimated age over 100 years, 24 inches (61 cm). *below*

Japanese white pine

Japanese white pine, late March, estimated age over 120 years, 38 inches (97 cm).
below

Japanese white pine, late March, estimated age over 80 years, 28 inches (70 cm).
right

Index

NOTE: Numbers in italics indicate pages where the entry is a secondary plant in a bonsai arrangement and does not appear as a main heading, but receives mention in either the text or the caption.

Water horsetail, 80
Water lily, 66
Weeping willow, 93
Welsh onion flower, 111

White pine, Japanese, 151–53
Wild grape, 109
Willow
    Virginia, 22
    Weeping, 93
Wisteria. *See Natsu-fuji; Sakko-fuji.*
    Japanese, 44–45.

Yamadori-shida (a type of osmunda), 26–27
Yamakobashi (a type of laurel), 99

Zelkova, Japanese, 120–21
Zumi (a type of crabapple), 20, 119